The Man Who Measured the World

Story by Wendy Macdonald
Illustrations by Vasja Koman

The Man Who Measured the World

Text: Wendy Macdonald
Illustrations: Vasja Koman
Editor: Angelique Campbell-Muir
Design: Leigh Ashforth
Reprint: Siew Han Ong

PM Extras Chapter Books
Sapphire Level 29 Set A
The Bommyknocker Tree
The Man Who Measured the World
Eric's Thai Travel Diary
H for Horrible
Jungle Trek
Lizard Tongue

Text © 2004 Wendy Macdonald
Illustrations © 2004 Cengage Learning Australia Pty Limited

Copyright Notice
This Work is copyright. No part of this Work may be reproduced, stored in a retrieval system, or transmitted in any form or by any means without prior written permission of the Publisher. Except as permitted under the Copyright Act 1968, for example any fair dealing for the purposes of private study, research, criticism or review, subject to certain limitations. These limitations include: Restricting the copying to a maximum of one chapter or 10% of this book, whichever is greater; Providing an appropriate notice and warning with the copies of the Work disseminated; Taking all reasonable steps to limit access to these copies to people authorised to receive these copies; Ensuring you hold the appropriate Licences issued by the Copyright Agency Limited ("CAL"), supply a remuneration notice to CAL and pay any required fees.

ISBN 978 0 17 011714 2
ISBN 978 0 17 011709 8 (set)

Cengage Learning Australia
Level 7, 80 Dorcas Street
South Melbourne, Victoria Australia 3205
Phone: 1300 790 853

Cengage Learning New Zealand
Unit 4B Rosedale Office Park
331 Rosedale Road, Albany, North Shore NZ 0632
Phone: 0508 635 766

For learning solutions, visit **cengage.com.au**

Printed in China by 1010 Printing International Ltd
11 15

Contents

CHAPTER 1 — The King's Idea — 4

CHAPTER 2 — A Bucket Full of Sunshine — 9

CHAPTER 3 — Marking the Days — 14

CHAPTER 4 — The Greatest Discovery — 22

CHAPTER 5 — The Prize — 29

CHAPTER 1

The King's Idea

'Look, Daddy!' exclaimed Xenia. 'Here comes the Royal Barge.'

Xenia and her father Eratosthenes were standing on the bank of the river Nile. Behind them were the marble columns of the Temple of Jupiter. The Temple of Jupiter contained the great library where Eratosthenes was the third librarian.

The Royal Barge was pulling in to shore, and people were streaming out of the library and up on the steps to welcome the King.

The King's Idea

The prow and stern of the Royal Barge were shaped like lotus flowers and were covered with gold leaf that gleamed in the sun. In the middle was an open cabin with purple curtains and a couch piled up with purple cushions for the King to rest on. There was an orchestra on board, which played sweet music, and a banquet table set with lovely food and big jugs of wine. Eight sturdy rowers wearing linen skirts and beaded collars pulled smoothly in time making the Barge glide in towards the library steps. Slaves ran to tie it up to the mooring posts.

Xenia stared open-mouthed at all this.

'Oh, Father,' she whispered. 'Wouldn't it be lovely to have a ride in that? Just imagine what fun it would be!'

Eratosthenes laughed. 'You can see just as much from a row-boat,' he said.

Xenia slipped down to have a closer look at the Barge while librarians, scholars, courtiers and other people crowded round to welcome the King.

The Man Who Measured the World

All the people of Alexandria were very proud of their library. It was begun by the King's grandfather, King Ptolemy 1. He ordered his learned men to gather or copy all the books of knowledge they could find so that scholars and wise men would have the information they wanted in one place, instead of having to search for it in many different places. The library now contained over 400 000 scrolls of papyrus, rolled on long rods with gilded ends.

As well as assembling the books, the King sent out far and wide for learned men to come to Alexandria to study these books. So Eratosthenes and Xenia had come to Egypt from Cyrene.

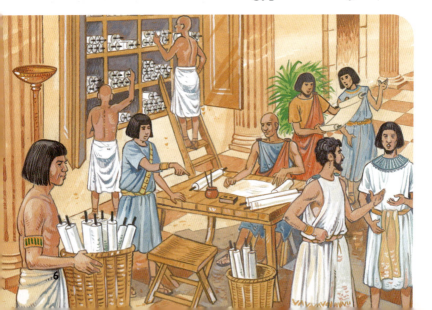

The King's Idea

The King was very proud of the library and liked to stroll through it and chat to the scholars who worked there.

Inside the library the King sat on a special throne and all the people gathered around to listen to him. Two attendants fanned him with fans made of peacock feathers to make a breeze and shoo the flies away. Xenia sat on the floor behind a pillar and hoped no one would notice her. The marble pavement was nice and cool and it had little pictures of birds and fish and flowers inlaid in it.

'I have had an idea,' announced the King. Everyone listened respectfully. 'Here,' he said, waving his hand at the collection of scrolls around him, 'we have the greatest collection of knowledge, and here,' and he waved his hand at the assembled wise men, 'are the wisest men in the world.'

All the scholars smirked at this and Xenia smiled at her father. But Eratosthenes just frowned and shuffled his sandals.

'I wish to give a prize,' the King went on, 'to the person who, in the next year, makes what is judged by you all to be the greatest scientific discovery. The prize will be a gold necklace, which I will personally present to the winner, and a journey in the Royal Barge.'

Everyone began to cheer and clap and to say how wise and good the King was, but Xenia only gave a deep gasp. A journey on the Royal Barge! Imagine it! Listening to the orchestra as the hippopotamuses splashed among the reeds… the pyramids slipping by… all the people waving… it would be wonderful!

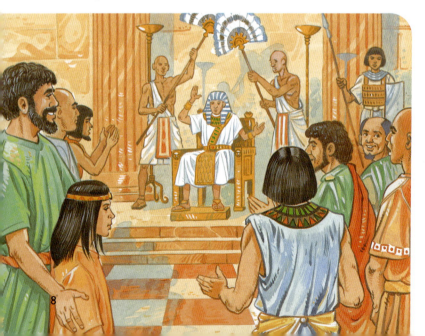

CHAPTER 2

A Bucket Full of Sunshine

At home that night Xenia asked, 'What are you going to discover for the King's competition, Father?'

'I don't know,' said Eratosthenes. 'It must be something important. Something no one has ever done before. All the others are talking about it.' Eratosthenes paused for a moment, then continued. 'I thought of counting the stars. No one has ever done that.'

Xenia laughed.

'No one *can* do that,' she said sleepily, and she closed her eyes and dreamed of counting the scrolls in the library, but they all turned into stars and swam away.

The next day, Eratosthenes had to go to the shipyards to see how the King's galleys were coming on. He and Xenia climbed to the top of the lighthouse. Xenia could see the shore with all the wharves and ships, and the sea stretching away into the furthest distance.

'How far does the sea go, Father?' she asked.

Eratosthenes shook his head.

'No one knows,' he said, 'but it must go for a very long way. Some say it goes right around the world.'

'But how far is that?' asked Xenia.

Eratosthenes looked at the horizon.

'No one knows that either,' he said.

The sun was setting and the shadow of the lighthouse stretched out to sea.

A Bucket Full of Sunshine

'If you knew that, you would win the King's competition, wouldn't you?' said Xenia.

Eratosthenes just nodded and said nothing.

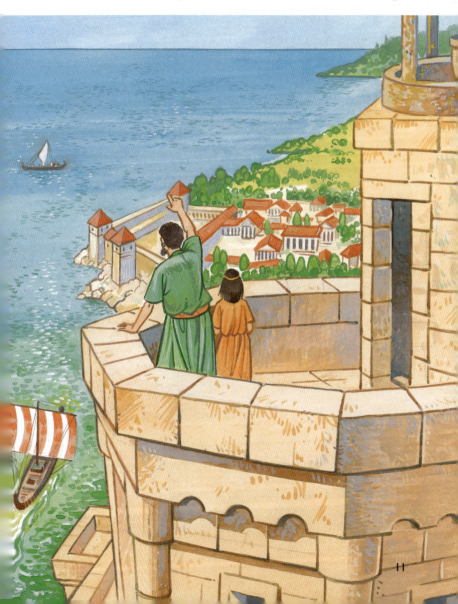

When they came home the water pot was empty. Xenia went to the well to draw some water, and Eratosthenes came too because Xenia was too little to pull up the heavy bucket herself. Xenia watched the bucket fall. It was dark at the bottom of the well and small ferns and mosses grew on the walls.

'It's very dark down there,' she said. 'The sun never gets to the bottom.'

'Last year, when I was at Aswan,' said her father, 'the sun shone straight down the well in the courtyard at the inn. I saw it.'

'You could have had a bucket full of sunshine,' said Xenia.

'I wanted a bucket full of water,' said her father. 'It was the hottest time of year, just about now, and the sun was right overhead.'

'Well that never happens here,' said Xenia, 'because we have to draw water every day and I look down every time.' And when she pulled up the bucket there was a fat green frog sitting on the rim.

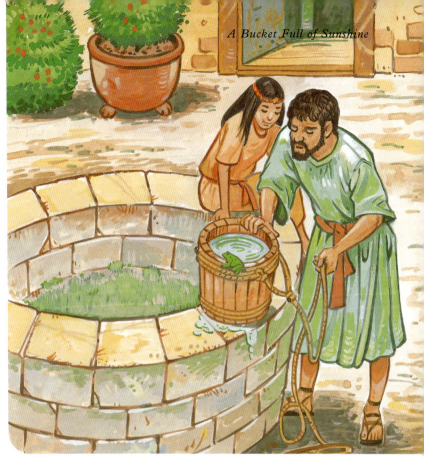

A Bucket Full of Sunshine

That night when Xenia was asleep, Eratosthenes took a piece of charcoal from the kitchen fire and began to draw on the kitchen table. First he drew part of a big circle, then he drew a little spot off to one side of it. He sat at the table for a long time, drawing lines and scribbling them out, until at last he rubbed away all his drawings and went to bed.

CHAPTER 3
Marking the Days

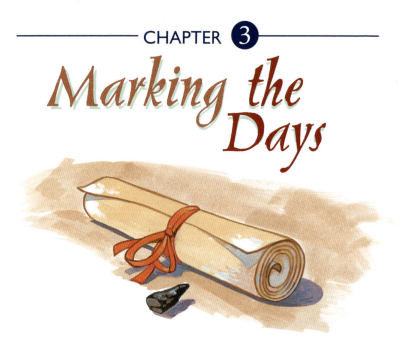

The next day, Xenia's friend Nefer came bouncing in to say that her family was going to make a trip up the Nile to Aswan, and could Xenia come too? Aswan was a long way from Alexandria but it was a very important place. At Aswan there were large quarries where the big blocks of stone for the Royal Tombs were cut. Nefer's father was in charge of one of these buildings and he had to see that the blocks of stone were loaded onto barges and floated down the river.

Marking the Days

Eratosthenes looked at his calendar.

'I want you to go to Aswan with Nefer,' he said to Xenia, 'because I want you to help me to win the King's competition. Will you do something for me?'

Xenia clapped her hands. 'Of course I will,' she said.

'I will give you something to take with you,' her father went on. He took a long strip of papyrus and spread it out on the table. On it he drew a series of squares. Like this.

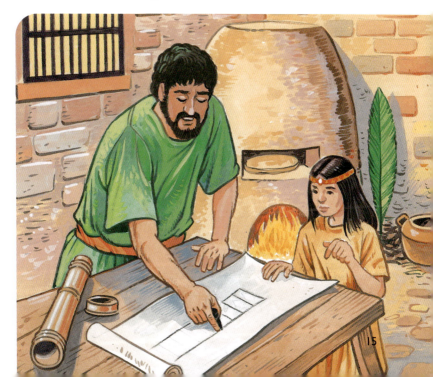

'Now,' he said to Xenia, 'every day, from the day you leave, you are to put a tick in one of these squares. And when you get to Aswan you are to look in the well every day.'

Xenia looked puzzled.

'One day, and only one day,' Eratosthenes continued, 'the sun will shine right to the bottom of the well. On that day you are to draw a picture of the sun in the square, like this,' and he showed her.

Xenia nodded.

'After that, you are to put a tick in every square until you come home.'

'What if I run out of squares?' Xenia asked.

Marking the Days

'Make some more,' said her father. 'Then we will know exactly how long you have been away and on what day it was that the sun shone straight down. Do you understand?'

'I don't understand how this is going to win the King's prize,' said Xenia.

'I will explain when you come home,' said Eratosthenes. And with that, he rolled up the strip of papyrus and put it in a hollow piece of bamboo, along with a piece of charcoal.

'Father, how far is it to Aswan?' Xenia asked. 'It's a long way, isn't it?'

'A very long way,' said Eratosthenes. 'It takes a camel fifty days to get there and a camel travels at about 100 stadia a day, so Aswan is 5000 stadia away.'

'Fifty days!' exclaimed Xenia.

'Don't worry,' said her father. 'You will be sailing, which won't take so long – and you and Nefer will be having fun anyway. But you must not forget to mark the squares for me.'

'I won't,' Xenia assured him.

So the next day Xenia said goodbye to Eratosthenes, and she and Nefer and Nefer's family sailed all the way up through the Land of Egypt until they came to Aswan. And every day Xenia put a tick on her chart. And every day she looked down the well.

Eratosthenes was marking off the days, too. He knew that the summer solstice was coming, the longest day of the year when the sun was most nearly overhead.

In front of the Temple of Jupiter was an obelisk. This was a tall shaft of stone with a polished brass top that shone like gold in the sun. All down its sides was writing which said how great and powerful the King was. Eratosthenes went to the Keeper of the King's Works and asked him exactly how tall the obelisk was, and the keeper told him.

On the day of the solstice Eratosthenes was waiting beside the obelisk. At noon the tall obelisk cast a shadow. It was not a very long shadow, but Eratosthenes measured it carefully.

Marking the Days

'What are you doing?' laughed his friends. 'Measuring a shadow!'

But Eratosthenes only smiled and replied, 'Wait and see.'

Far away in Aswan, on the same day, Xenia looked down the well again. At noon the sun shone straight down to the very bottom. She ran to her piece of papyrus and drew a picture of the sun in the square.

That night Eratosthenes cleaned his kitchen table. Then he took a piece of charcoal and sharpened it to a point. Next he took his instruments and drew a long, thin triangle (a small version of the triangle made by the obelisk, the shadow and the sun's rays). When he had finished the drawing, he measured the angles with his protractor. The angle which the sun's rays made with the obelisk was 7.2 degrees.

When Xenia reached home she ran to her father and gave him her papyrus. Carefully he counted the squares, then he gave her a big hug. The sun had shone straight down the well at Aswan on the same day as he had measured the shadow.

Marking the Days

That night, Eratosthenes sat down at the kitchen table again and made his calculations. But he would not tell even Xenia what his discovery was.

CHAPTER 4
The Greatest Discovery

Months passed and at last it was time for the King to award his prize. The whole court was assembled in the throne room at the Royal Palace. The Queen was there with all her ladies, the courtiers wore their best clothes and all the wise men, astronomers, magicians and scholars were eagerly waiting to know who would win the prize.

One by one the wise men came forward to present their discoveries.

The Greatest Discovery

'Sire,' began Demetrius of Corinth. 'I have drawn up a catalogue of all the books in this library: their names, who wrote them, where they came from and how long they are. This immense work has taken me a whole year and I have laboured night and day to complete it.'

This was not true, for Demetrius had spent much of the time sleeping under a palm tree while his slaves and the other librarians did all the work.

'Hmmm,' said the King. 'Next.' He wanted something that would make his Kingdom famous throughout the world, not just a list of old books.

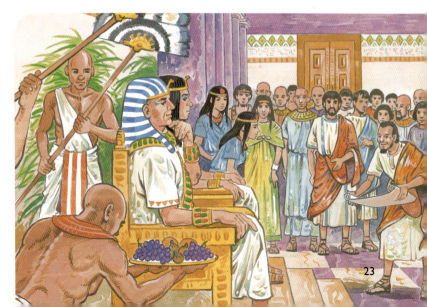

The Man Who Measured the World

The next candidate was the second librarian, Aristarchus of Rhodes. He bowed low to the King and said, 'Your majesty, I have counted every one of the scales of the crocodile. There are large scales, medium scales and small ones – and I have counted them all. And since the crocodile is one of the gods of Egypt, I propose that the number of scales is equal to the number of years that Your Majesty's Kingdom will endure.'

The Greatest Discovery

At this Eratosthenes gave a snort of laughter and the others said angrily, 'Hush!'

The King was very pleased with this idea because he wanted his Kingdom to last for a long time. So he smiled and said, 'Very good! Very good, Aristarchus! Stand over there,' and he gestured to a place of honour at his right hand.

Now it was Eratosthenes' turn. He took a deep breath and stepped forward.

'Your Majesty,' he said, 'I have calculated the circumference of the Earth.'

There was an astonished silence then the King and all the courtiers burst out laughing.

'No one can do that,' said the King. 'What did you use for a measuring tape?'

'The sun was my measuring tape,' said Eratosthenes, 'and this is how I did it.'

Everyone stopped laughing and listened.

The Man Who Measured the World

'We know the Earth is a big round ball,' said Eratosthenes. 'Let Your Majesty be the sun.' The King looked pleased.

Eratosthenes took one of the guards and stood him at the back of the hall right in front of the King. 'This man,' he said, 'is the well in the courtyard of the inn at Aswan.'

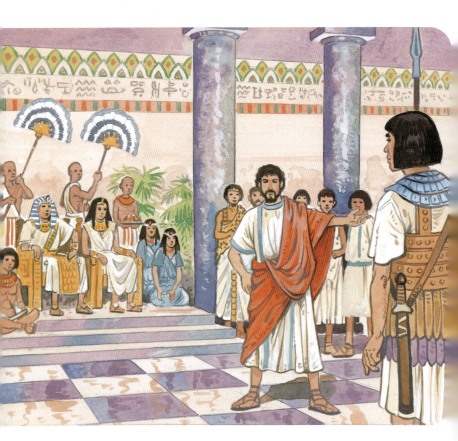

Then he took another man and stood him at the far side of the hall. 'This man is the obelisk in front of the Temple here in Alexandria,' he said.

'Now at noon of the summer solstice Your Majesty's sublime face shines directly down the well at Aswan and, at the same time, the obelisk here in Alexandria casts a shadow of 7.2 degrees,' Eratosthenes began to explain.

'Now the sun is a very long way away, so far that we can assume its rays are parallel. We can imagine one ray shining from the sun directly down the well at Aswan, and another shining from the sun just passing the top of the obelisk and striking the ground at the end of the obelisk's shadow at Alexandria. The angle between the top of the obelisk and this ray is 7.2 degrees. If we draw an imaginary line down from the well at Aswan to the centre of the Earth, and another down from the top of the obelisk at Alexandria to the centre of the Earth, they too will intersect at an angle of 7.2 degrees.' Eratosthenes paused before going on.

'Now, if we divide that angle (7.2) into the number of degrees in a circle (360), and multiply that by the distance between Alexandria and Aswan (5000 stadia), the result will be the circumference of the Earth. So, 7.2 divides into 360 fifty times, and fifty multiplied by 5000 is 250 000. Therefore, the circumference of the Earth must be 250 000 stadia.'

He stopped talking but the hall was quiet. No one could think of anything to say. Eratosthenes bowed to the King.

'Of all that vast distance, Your Majesty's glorious Kingdom occupies no less that one fiftieth,' Eratosthenes told the King. The King thought that this was far too small and he frowned, but Eratosthenes went on. 'No other king knows the size of his kingdom relative to the size of the Earth, and no other king,' and at this point Eratosthenes bowed even more deeply, 'knows the circumference of the Earth.'

CHAPTER 5

The Prize

At this, a babble of talk broke out among the wise men, and the second librarian, who was very angry at having his crocodile scales ignored, snapped, 'No one can prove what you have said. My count of crocodile scales can be proven.'

'Anyone can prove what I have said,' said Eratosthenes. 'And I put it to all the learned men assembled here to show that there is a flaw in my argument.' At this, all the wise men began to argue even louder than before, but they had to agree that Eratosthenes' reasoning was correct.

The Man Who Measured the World

At last the King stood up and clapped his hands for silence. He declared that Eratosthenes had won the prize. Eratosthenes came forward and the King clasped a splendid gold necklace around his neck and said, 'The Royal Barge is at your disposal tomorrow.'

So Xenia got to travel in the Royal Barge. She bounced on the purple cushions, conducted the orchestra and ate all the honey cakes she wanted. Eratosthenes wore his gold necklace and all the people on the bank waved and said, 'There goes the man who measured the world.'

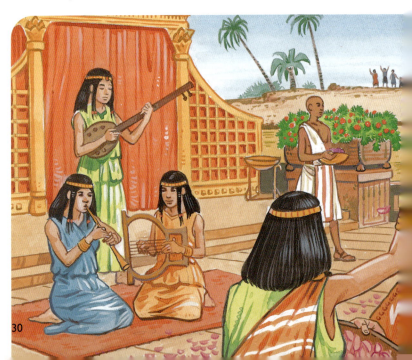

The Prize

As they came home Xenia asked her father, 'What are we going to do next father? Measuring the Earth was fun.'

Up above, the stars were coming out. Eratosthenes smiled.

'I am going to count the stars in the sky,' he said. The head boatman laughed.

'No one can do that,' he said.

'My father can,' Xenia declared. 'He is the cleverest man in the world. The King himself says so.'

The Man Who Measured the World

Eratosthenes' method of calculating the size of the Earth was correct, but we don't know what his figure was because no one today knows the exact length of a stadium. The modern measurement of the circumference of the Earth is 39 843.2 kilometres, or 24 902 miles.

Eratosthenes made many more mathematical discoveries and he did prepare a catalogue of the stars.